Our Joke Writing Book

A Fun Activity to Do With Dad, with 30 Themes, Creative Prompts and Puns

by Velma Minosa

How to Use This Book

Each page has a dad related theme, and 2 prompts to get you started. The first question is for coming up with a funny story, and the second question is for using your imaginations to take it one step further into potential hilariousness.

Next, try to come up with puns or word plays related to the theme or story. Three examples are given on the opposite page to inspire you to come up with your own.

Tip: Think of funny unexpected connections between 2 different characters, things or ideas.

The final joke can be in any form, as long as it has a setup and a punch line.

The opposite page has some sample puns (for older kids), and blank space for brainstorming, sketching, or making notes for future related jokes.

Just have fun and adapt it to any age from 8 to adult. Feel free to be witty, corny, clever, silly, absurd or just plain goofy.

"I'm on a roll with these burgers."

"Let's ketchup at the grill."

"Flipping out at the BBQ."

Brainstorm

Grilling

Start with... Imagine a funny situation when Dad is at the BBQ.

_____

_____

_____

What if... there was a missing burger?

_____

_____

_____

Characters   Puns

THE JOKE

Setup

Punchline

"Fishing for compliments."

"Hooked on fishing."

"Catch you later!"

Brainstorm

Fishing

Start with... What's funny about fishing with Dad?

_____

_____

_____

What if... a fish commented on his hat?

_____

_____

_____

Characters   Puns

THE JOKE

Setup

- -

Punchline

"I've got a screw loose."

"Tooling around."

"I'm nuts about bolts."

Brainstorm

Mr. Fix-It

Start with... Think of what can go ridiculously wrong when Dad is trying to fix something.

_____

_____

_____

What if... a pet got involved?

_____

_____

_____

Characters

Puns

THE JOKE

Setup

- -

Punchline

"That's how I roll."

"Cheer pressure."

GOGOGO!

"Fan-tastic dad."

Brainstorm

Sports

Start with... What's a funny thing Dad might say at a sports game?

_____

_____

_____

What if... someone thought he said something else?

_____

_____

_____

Characters   Puns

THE JOKE

Setup

- -

Punchline

"Wheel proud of this ride."

"Revving about it."

"Dad's hot wheel deal."

Brainstorm

Cars

Start with... What is the coolest thing about Dad's car?

_____

_____

_____

What if... something unexpected made that cool thing suddenly embarrassing?

_____

_____

_____

Characters

Puns

THE JOKE

Setup

- -

Punchline

"Mower the merrier."

"Lawn and order."

"Mow problems, mow solutions."

Brainstorm

Lawn Care

Start with... Does the lawn and Dad's hair ever get overgrown
at the same time?

_____

_____

_____

What if... both got cut on the same day, but a little too much?

_____

_____

_____

Characters

Puns

THE JOKE

Setup

- -

Punchline

"Lost but not least."

"Branching out with dad."

"Pitching a fit."

Brainstorm

Camping

Start with... What hilarious thing has happened or might happen on a camping trip with Dad?

_____

_____

_____

What if... there was a leak in something?

_____

_____

_____

Characters   Puns

THE JOKE

Setup

Punchline

"Dressed to impress, no less."

"Suit yourself!"

"Cooler than the weather."

Brainstorm

Clothes

Start with... What item of clothing would Dad hate to lose?

_____

_____

_____

What if... someone found it, and wore it in front of him?

_____

_____

_____

Characters   Puns

THE JOKE

Setup

- -

Punchline

"Chordially invited."

"Dad's garage band is more garage, less band."

"Treble maker."

Brainstorm

Music

Start with... What would happen if Dad's favorite band came to the house and asked him to sing a song with them?

_____

_____

_____

What if... the wierd neighbor came over?

_____

_____

_____

Characters   Puns

THE JOKE

Setup

- -

Punchline

"Whisk-taker in the kitchen."

"Chef of the day, every day."

"Decree a la carte."

Brainstorm

Superhero

Start with... If Dad has a superpower for cooking, what would be the type of food?

_____

_____

_____

What if... he ordered this in too much detail at a restaurant ?

_____

_____

_____

Characters   Puns

THE JOKE

Setup

- -

Punchline

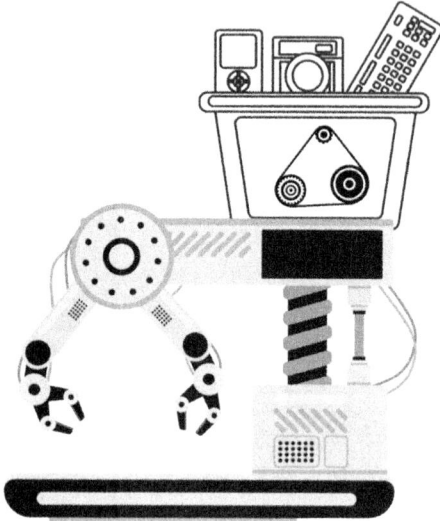

"Tech it easy, Dad!"

"Dad's drawer of dormant devices."

"Geared up for fun."

Brainstorm

Gadgets

Start with... What is the most unused gadget Dad has in the house?

_____

_____

_____

What if... someone came over and asked to borow it?

_____

_____

_____

Characters

Puns

THE JOKE

Setup

- -

Punchline

"Reel fun."

"Film-flam."

"Scene it all."

Brainstorm

Movies

Start with... What character in a funny movie would Dad be great at playing?

_____

_____

_____

What if... something happened in public and he started acting like that character?

_____

_____

_____

Characters

Puns

THE JOKE

Setup

- -

Punchline

"Brew-tiful morning"

"Rush hour at home."

"Scramble the plans."

Brainstorm

Morning Routine

Start with... What's the funniest part about Dad getting ready in the morning?

_____

_____

_____

What if... his routine was disrupted by something ridiculous?

_____

_____

_____

Characters   Puns

THE JOKE

Setup

- -

Punchline

"Reach for the stars, even if you pull a muscle."

"Twist of fate."

"Flex-appeal!"

Brainstorm

Dancing

Start with... What is Dad's most unique dance move?

_____

_____

_____

What if... his boss or coworker caught him doing his dance
move at work?

_____

_____

_____

Characters

Puns

THE JOKE

Setup

- -

Punchline

"Don't look a gift horse in the mouth."

"Keep your eyes peeled."

"Hit the hay."

Brainstorm

Favorite Sayings

Start with... What is one of Dad's strangest phrases he uses?

_____

_____

_____

What if... someone thought he meant something entirely
different?

_____

_____

_____

Characters

Puns

THE JOKE

Setup

- -

Punchline

"Paws and relax."

"Purr-fect companion."

"Fur real?"

Brainstorm

Pets

Start with... What does Dad and his favorite pet have in common?

_____

_____

_____

What if... the pet could talk, what would it say to him?

_____

_____

_____

Characters   Puns

THE JOKE

Setup

Punchline

"Aisle be back."

"Cart-astrophe waiting to happen."

"Serial snacker."

Brainstorm

Grocery Shopping

Start with... Is there a snack Dad always buys that Mom says is not healthy?

_____

_____

_____

What if... What is his funniest excuse?

_____

_____

_____

Characters   Puns

THE JOKE

Setup

- -

Punchline

""nstant human, just add coffee."

"Bean there, brewed that."

"Mug-nificent mood enhancer."

Brainstorm

Coffee

Start with... What is Dad like before he has his morning coffee (or breakfast)?

_____

_____

_____

What if... a relative called just to chat about nothing important before he had his coffee or breakfast?

_____

_____

_____

Characters

Puns

THE JOKE

Setup

- -

Punchline

"Disguise the limit."

"Ghoul times ahead."

"Santa-mental value."

Brainstorm

Holidays

Start with... Does Dad have a silly costume he sometimes wears for holidays or other occasions?

_____

_____

_____

What if... there was a sticky note someone put on the back that he didn't notice?

_____

_____

_____

Characters   Puns

THE JOKE

Setup

- -

Punchline

"The generation game gap."

"Virtual reality check."

"Level up your life."

Brainstorm

Gaming

Start with... What game does dad always win, and why is it funny?

_____

_____

_____

What if... someone gave him a funny award certificate, what would it say he was "World's Best" at?

_____

_____

_____

Characters   Puns

THE JOKE

Setup

- -

Punchline

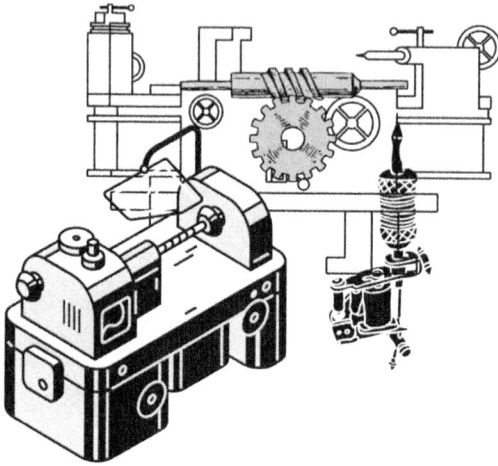

"Machine learning curve."

"Gearing up."

"Torque of the town."

Brainstorm

Machines

Start with... What machine does Dad love to tinker with the most?

_____

_____

_____

What if... it did something completely unexpected?

_____

_____

_____

Characters

Puns

THE JOKE

Setup

- -

Punchline

"Pasta point of no return."

"Chew on this."

"Fork it over."

Brainstorm

Eating Out

Start with... Did Dad ever make a funny mistake placing an order at a restaurant?

_____

_____

_____

What if... the workers also made a mistake with the same order, creating a huge confusion?

_____

_____

_____

Characters   Puns

THE JOKE

Setup

- -

Punchline

"Nailed it."

"DI-Why? Because I can!"

"Board meeting in the garage."

Brainstorm

DIY Projects

Start with... Has Dad had a DIY project go terribly wrong in a funny way?

_____

_____

_____

What if... a relative, friend or neighbor didn't know about this, and asked him to help them do the same project?

_____

_____

_____

Characters

Puns

THE JOKE

Setup

Punchline

"Zoom through work."

"Key-board meetings."

"Remote possibility."

meow!

Brainstorm

Work from Home

Start with... What's the funniest thing that happened while Dad was on a work call or Zoom?

_____

_____

_____

What if... he didn't realize the camera or mic was on?

_____

_____

_____

Characters

Puns

THE JOKE

Setup

- -

Punchline

"Couch surfing."

"Channeling my inner detective."

"Remote possibilities."

Brainstorm

TV

Start with... What funny thing happens when Dad can't find the remote?

_____

_____

_____

What if... he finds it in the most ridiculous spot?

_____

_____

_____

Characters   Puns

THE JOKE

Setup

- - - - - - - - - - - - - - - - - - - -

Punchline

"Escape key artist."

AARGH!!

"Reboot camp."

"Screen and shout."

Brainstorm

Computers

Start with... What does Dad say to his computer when he is frustrated with it?

_____

_____

_____

What if... it answered back with wierd, random sound effects and a voice?

_____

_____

_____

Characters   Puns

THE JOKE

Setup

- -

Punchline

"Driving me crazy."

"Driven to succeed."

LET'S GO

ADVENTURE

"Fuel good."

Brainstorm

Driving

Start with... What's funny about road trips with dad?

_____

_____

_____

What if... he sings while driving, but makes up lyrics to songs
he thinks he knows?

_____

_____

_____

Characters

Puns

THE JOKE

Setup

- -

Punchline

"Crew-tique session."

"Project playdate."

"Colleague collage."

Brainstorm

Friends

Start with... How does Dad describe his friends from work?

_____

_____

_____

What if... they came over for dinner and were very different from how he described?

_____

_____

_____

Characters   Puns

THE JOKE

Setup

Punchline

"Youth or consequences."

"Kiddy capers."

"Joke of all trades."

Brainstorm

Childhood Stories

Start with... What's the funniest story Dad tells from his
childhood?

_____

_____

_____

What if... Grandma had a very different version?

_____

_____

_____

Characters

Puns

THE JOKE

Setup

- -

Punchline

"Ballooning expectations."

"Party animal control."

"Cake-walk in the park."

Brainstorm

Birthday Parties

Start with... How does Dad like to make birthday parties memorable?

_____

_____

_____

What if... it became unforgettable in a hilariously unexpected way?

_____

_____

_____

Characters

Puns

THE JOKE

Setup

Punchline

HAHAHA

I hope you have enjoyed this book and shared many laughs. Please consider leaving a review on Amazon.com. Thank you!

Printed in Great Britain
by Amazon

43039665R00036